The Ladies' Book of Baking

First published in 2013
LOVE FOOD is an imprint of Parragon Books Ltd

Parragon
Chartist House
15–17 Trim Street
Bath, BA1 1HA, UK

ISBN: 978-1-4723-1108-5

Printed in China

Project managed by **Annabel King**
Designed by **Lisa McCormick**
Cover illustration by **Catharine Collingridge** www.catharinecollingridge.co.uk
New photography by **Sian Irvine**
Introduction and additional text by **Anna-Marie Julyan**
New recipe text by **Christine McFadden**
Additional photography by **Henry Sparrow**

NOTES FOR THE READER

This book uses both metric and imperial measurements. Follow the same units of measurement
throughout; do not mix metric and imperial. All spoon measurements are level: teaspoons are assumed
to be 5 ml, and tablespoons are assumed to be 15 ml. Unless otherwise stated, milk is assumed to be
full fat, eggs and individual vegetables are medium, and pepper is freshly ground black pepper. Unless
otherwise stated, all root vegetables should be washed in plain water and peeled prior to using.

Garnishes, decorations and serving suggestions are all optional and not necessarily included in the recipe
ingredients or method. The times given are an approximate guide only. Preparation times differ according
to the techniques used by different people and the cooking times may also vary from those given.
Optional ingredients, variations or serving suggestions have not been included in the time calculations.

Recipes using raw or very lightly cooked eggs should be avoided by infants, the elderly, pregnant women,
convalescents and anyone suffering from an illness. Pregnant and breastfeeding women are advised
to avoid eating peanuts and peanut products. Sufferers from nut allergies should be aware that
some of the ready-made ingredients used in the recipes in this book may contain nuts. Always
check the packaging before use. Vegetarians should be aware that some of the ready-made
ingredients used in the recipes in this book may contain animal products.
Always check the packaging before use.

Introduction

Baking has officially come out of the closet, or, to be precise, the cupboard. Where once a passion for creating finely iced fancies was at best old-fashioned, the trend for home baking means we can once again make a song and dance in the kitchen, invite friends around and, yes, even throw tea parties.

What a relief there's no need to go on pretending, because the truth is that ladies love baking. The trend for cupcakes, muffins, whoopie pies and tarts of every hue, flavour and style has got us reaching for our piping bags, scouring websites for vintage china and coveting cake stands.

Where once ladies gathered to take tea and enjoy cake baked by the cook, modern ladies are the cooks. This gives us the added bonus of learning a lifelong talent for keeping loved ones in freshly baked buns. (Not to be underestimated.)

With over 50 recipes to choose from, *The Ladies' Book of Baking* is intended as a source of inspiration, both for the type of cake or pastry to serve and how to display the finished result. Beautiful baking doesn't finish in the kitchen. Matching your recipe to the occasion, serving it with a little flair and imagination, then watching people enjoy is as important as mixing the ingredients together in the first place.

A trend for miniature cakes demonstrates that these days we really do like to have our cake and eat it (to ourselves). Thinking practically, however, it provides an opportunity to experiment with flavours, finishing with something that appears more intricate and complicated than it is.

Think of mini Mango Cakes with a light dusting of icing sugar, classic Victoria sponge mixture baked in a mini muffin tray or small Caramelized Apple Tarts. Better than giant cookies or ten-tiered cakes, they provide a taste of heaven without blowing your sugar intake for the entire week on one treat.

What is it about this baking that makes it so popular? Ultimately, baking is comforting – from turning the much-thumbed pages of your favourite recipes to the warm smell of spiced apple pie muffins in the oven. If you're being thrifty, baking is a way of saving money, while increasingly people are realizing that home baking is not some impossible task best approached with caution and a hotline to your nearest supermarket bakery. If you start with straightforward recipes and build a repertoire gradually, your confidence and abilities will grow.

A NOTE ON INGREDIENTS:

Flour, essential to so much baking, is always best stored somewhere cool and dry. If you tend to bake in bursts with long, fallow periods, then remember to check the best before date. Bear in mind that butter gives a better flavour than vegetable fat or margarine, but will often need to be softened before you begin – the lowest setting on your microwave is handy if you forgot to take it out in advance. Eggs should be at room temperature and fruit is best unwaxed. You'll find that caster sugar gives a smoother texture than granulated.

GENERAL TIPS:

This book covers pastry, classic cakes, cookies, family bakes and ideas for different occasions. Of course, as you become familiar with a recipe you might decide to tweak it, but as a general rule it's a good idea to read a recipe all the way through before beginning. Some cooks advise weighing all the ingredients beforehand, but if that's not your style just make sure you've read ahead and sally forth in your own style – let's face it, some cooks are simply messier than others. At least a smudge of icing on your forehead shows you're not afraid to get stuck in.

It's always a good idea to start by preheating the oven and preparing whatever tin you are using before you begin. Unless you're chilling pastry or leaving bread dough to rise, don't leave mixtures standing; get them in the oven baking. Certainly when it comes to classic cakes and pastries, accuracy is important, but as you bake more you'll learn where you can tweak a recipe.

If you're throwing a party or someone important is coming to tea, it's probably worth baking a recipe you're familiar with and giving that triple-layered chocolate confection shaped like a swan a miss, for now at least.

Once you've mastered the basics, you can start to think about the endless options for presentation. The trend for all things vintage is fantastic if your style is eclectic, as is a talent for collecting mismatched china. Save tins at Christmas and look for items like old hat boxes, which can be stacked to raise cakes to different levels, making them more eye-catching. It all depends on the occasion.

Equally, you may wish to stick with a more traditional style, using classic white linen on the table and dressing the table properly. A wealth of icing and decorating paraphernalia in shops makes it much easier to decorate cakes without getting icing sugar everywhere, allowing you to combine the best of traditional baking methods with modern bake and icing ware.

A little bit of forward planning and a few simple techniques will have you turning out beautiful cakes that fit the occasion and impress every time, making you proud to be hostess. Take your time, relax and enjoy being a lady with absolutely no need for a cook, because actually it's so much more fun doing it yourself.

Let *The Ladies' Book of Baking* be your gentle guide to turning out the most delicious pies, pastries, cakes and bakes and presenting them in your own inimitable style. Whether you're catering for a party, baking for your family or even just for yourself, follow the hints and tips in this book and you shouldn't go far wrong. Remember that your cakes will be individual because they were made by you. It's the love and care put into each batch that gives the most joy to those who eat them and to you as cook.

Afternoon Tea

Afternoon Tea

We have Anna, 7th Duchess of Bedford, to thank for coming up with the ritual of afternoon tea, when one afternoon in 1840 she tinkled her bell to request that a tray of tea, bread, butter and cake be brought to her room. Unfortunately times change and ring your bell hard as you might, a certain amount of forward planning, baking and brewing is now required for the same result.

In our hectic modern world treat the occasion as a valuable opportunity to stop the clock (somewhere between 4–5pm), spend time with good friends and spread a little cheer. Of course, just how you play it is a matter of personal preference. By the Edwardian era, afternoon tea was quite the social occasion, replete with intricate tea services and a system of anxiously meted out etiquette.

Unless you are a duchess, it might be simpler to follow a few simple rules: Arrange the cake stand with finger sandwiches on the bottom tier, scones in the middle and delicate cakes on top. The hostess is in charge of pouring tea, unless there are more than a table-full of guests, in which case nominate a couple of friends to help. Add milk to the poured tea and refrain from clinking the teaspoon noisily. Hold both cup and saucer unless seated. There is no need to stick one's pinkie in the air and under absolutely no circumstance dunk biscuits.

The 'rules' are, of course, open to interpretation, because this is your event, but one piece of advice worth remembering is to plan ahead and this equipment list is a good place to start:

Airtight tea caddy
Teapot
Urn or metal jug for hot water
Teacups and saucers
Dessert plates
Dessert forks
Butter knives
Teaspoons
Tea strainer and holder
Milk jug
Napkins (ideally linen)
Tablecloth
Sugar bowl with spoon or tongs
Cake stand
Cake plate
Tray

HOW TO MAKE THE PERFECT CUP OF TEA:

Fill your kettle with freshly drawn water and just before it reaches the boil, swirl some hot water in your teapot then discard. Use one heaped teaspoon of tea leaves per person plus one for the pot. Pour boiling water over the top and allow the tea to stand for 3–6 minutes, depending on the size of tealeaf. Give the pot a good stir before pouring through a strainer into cups. Add cold, fresh milk to taste.

Mini Victoria Sandwich Cakes

MAKES 12

PREP TIME 20 mins, plus cooling

COOK TIME 15 mins

Ingredients

70 g/2½ oz lightly salted butter, softened, plus extra for greasing

70 g/2½ oz caster sugar

70 g/2½ oz self-raising flour

1 egg

1 egg yolk

1 tsp vanilla extract

DECORATION

150 ml/5 fl oz double cream

6 tbsp strawberry jam

85 g/3 oz icing sugar

1 tbsp lemon juice

Method

1 Preheat the oven to 180°C/350°F/ Gas Mark 4. Grease and base-line a 12-hole mini muffin tin. Put the butter, caster sugar, flour, egg, egg yolk and vanilla in a mixing bowl and beat together with an electric handheld whisk until it is smooth and creamy.

2 Using a teaspoon, spoon the mixture into the muffin tin sections and level with the back of the spoon. Bake in the preheated oven for 15 minutes, or until risen and just firm to the touch. Leave in the tray for 5 minutes, then transfer to a wire rack to cool.

3 For the decoration, whip the cream until it just peaks. Split the cakes in half horizontally using a small serrated knife. Press 2 tablespoons of the jam through a small sieve into a bowl to extract the seeds. Put the sieved jam in a small paper piping bag and snip off the tip. Sandwich the cakes together with the remaining jam and cream.

4 Beat the icing sugar and lemon juice together in a bowl until smooth. Spoon the icing over the cakes, spreading it just to the edges. Pipe dots of jam on top of each cake and draw a wooden skewer through them.

Frosted Carrot Cake

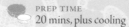

SERVES
16

PREP TIME
20 mins, plus cooling

COOK TIME
40–45 mins

Ingredients

175 ml/6 fl oz sunflower oil, plus extra for greasing

175 g/6 oz light muscovado sugar

3 eggs, beaten

175 g/6 oz grated carrots

85 g/3 oz sultanas

55 g/2 oz walnut pieces

grated rind of 1 orange

175 g/6 oz self-raising flour

1 tsp bicarbonate of soda

1 tsp ground cinnamon

½ tsp grated nutmeg

strips of orange zest, to decorate

FROSTING

200 g/7 oz full-fat soft cheese

100 g/3½ oz icing sugar

2 tsp orange juice

Method

1 Preheat the oven to 180°C/350°F/ Gas Mark 4. Grease and line the base of a 23-cm/9-inch square cake tin.

2 In a large bowl beat together the oil, muscovado sugar and eggs. Stir in the grated carrots, sultanas, walnuts and orange rind.

3 Sift together the flour, bicarbonate of soda, cinnamon and nutmeg, then stir evenly into the carrot mixture.

4 Spoon the mixture into the prepared cake tin and bake in the preheated oven for 40–45 minutes, until well risen and firm to the touch.

5 Remove the cake from the oven and set on a wire rack for 5 minutes. Turn out onto the wire rack to cool completely.

6 For the frosting, combine the soft cheese, icing sugar and orange juice in a bowl and beat until smooth. Spread over the top of the cake and swirl with a palette knife. Decorate with strips of orange zest and serve cut into squares.

2

4

6

Rich Fruit Cake

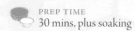

SERVES 16 **PREP TIME** 30 mins, plus soaking **COOK TIME** 2¼–2¾ hrs

Ingredients

350 g/12 oz sultanas

225 g/8 oz raisins

115 g/4 oz ready-to-eat dried apricots, chopped

85 g/3 oz stoned dates, chopped

4 tbsp dark rum or brandy (optional)

finely grated rind and juice of 1 orange

225 g/8 oz unsalted butter, softened, plus extra for greasing

225 g/8 oz light muscovado sugar

4 eggs, beaten

70 g/2½ oz chopped mixed peel

85 g/3 oz glacé cherries, quartered

25 g/1 oz chopped glacé ginger or stem ginger

40 g/1½ oz blanched almonds, chopped

200 g/7 oz plain flour

1 tsp ground mixed spice

Method

1 Place the sultanas, raisins, apricots and dates in a large bowl and stir in the rum, if using, orange rind and orange juice. Cover and leave to soak for several hours or overnight.

2 Preheat the oven to 150°C/300°F/ Gas Mark 2. Grease a 20-cm/ 8-inch round cake tin and line with baking paper.

3 Beat the butter and sugar together until pale and creamy. Gradually beat in the eggs, beating hard after each addition. Stir in the soaked fruits, mixed peel, glacé cherries, glacé ginger and blanched almonds.

4 Sift the flour and mixed spice, then fold lightly and evenly into the mixture. Spoon the mixture into the prepared cake tin and smooth the surface, making a slight depression in the centre with the back of the spoon.

5 Bake in the preheated oven for 2¼–2¾ hours, or until the cake is beginning to shrink away from the sides and a skewer inserted into the centre comes out clean. Cool completely in the tin.

6 Turn out the cake and remove the baking paper. Wrap in some greaseproof paper and foil, and store for at least two months before use.

1

3

3

Lemon Drizzle Cake

SERVES	PREP TIME	COOK TIME
12	20 mins, plus cooling	1 hour

Ingredients

2 eggs

175 g/6 oz caster sugar

150 g/5½ oz soft margarine, plus extra for greasing

finely grated rind of 1 lemon

175 g/6 oz self-raising flour

125 ml/4 fl oz milk

icing sugar, for dusting

SYRUP

140 g/5 oz icing sugar

50 ml/2 fl oz fresh lemon juice

Method

1 Preheat the oven to 180°C/350°F/ Gas Mark 4. Grease an 18-cm/7-inch square cake tin and line with baking paper.

2 Place the eggs, caster sugar and margarine in a mixing bowl and beat hard until smooth and fluffy. Stir in the lemon rind, then fold in the flour lightly and evenly. Stir in the milk, mixing evenly, then spoon into the prepared cake tin, smoothing level.

3 Bake in the preheated oven for 45–50 minutes, or until golden brown and firm to the touch. Remove from the oven and stand the tin on a wire rack.

4 To make the syrup, place the icing sugar and lemon juice in a small saucepan and heat gently, stirring until the sugar dissolves. Do not boil.

5 Prick the warm cake all over with a skewer, and spoon the hot syrup evenly over the top, allowing it to be absorbed.

6 Leave to cool completely in the tin, then turn out the cake, cut into 12 pieces and dust with a little icing sugar before serving.

Cherry & Almond Loaves

MAKES
12

PREP TIME
15 mins, plus cooling

COOK TIME
25 mins

Ingredients

85 g/3 oz lightly salted butter,
softened, plus extra for greasing

70 g/2½ oz caster sugar

1 egg

1 egg yolk

70 g/2½ oz self-raising flour

½ tsp almond extract

55 g/2 oz ground almonds

55 g/2 oz natural glacé cherries

2 tbsp flaked almonds

55 g/2 oz icing sugar

2 tsp lemon juice

Method

1 Preheat the oven to 180°C/350°F/ Gas Mark 4. Grease and base-line 12 individual loaf tins. Put the butter, caster sugar, egg, egg yolk, flour, almond extract and ground almonds in a mixing bowl and beat together with an electric handheld whisk until smooth and creamy. Chop the cherries and stir in.

2 Using a teaspoon, spoon the mixture into the trays and level with the back of the spoon. Break up the flaked almonds slightly by squeezing them in your hands and scatter them over the cake mixture. Bake in the preheated oven for 25 minutes, or until risen and just firm to the touch. Leave in the tray for 5 minutes, then transfer to a wire rack to cool.

3 Beat the icing sugar and lemon juice together in a small bowl and drizzle over the cakes with a teaspoon. Leave to set.

Mango Cakes

 MAKES
12

PREP TIME
15 mins, plus soaking

COOK TIME
25 mins

Ingredients

70 g/2½ oz dried mango,
finely chopped

finely grated rind of 1 orange,
plus 3 tbsp juice

25 g/1 oz creamed coconut

85 g/3 oz lightly salted butter,
softened, plus extra for greasing

70 g/2½ oz caster sugar

1 egg

85 g/3 oz self-raising flour

icing sugar, for dusting

Method

1 Preheat the oven to 180°C/350°F/
Gas Mark 4. Grease and base-line
12 individual loaf tins. Put the mango
and orange juice in a small bowl and
leave to stand, covered, for 2–3 hours,
or until the orange juice is mostly
absorbed. Finely grate the coconut
(if it's very firm and difficult to grate,
warm it briefly in the microwave first).

2 Put the coconut, butter, sugar, egg,
flour and orange rind in a mixing
bowl and beat together with an
electric handheld whisk until smooth
and pale. Stir in the mango and any
unabsorbed orange juice.

3 Using a teaspoon, spoon the mixture
into the trays and level with the back
of the spoon. Bake in the

preheated oven for 25 minutes, or
until risen and just firm to the touch.
Leave in the tray for 5 minutes, then
transfer to a wire rack to cool.

4 Serve lightly dusted with icing sugar.

Scones

 MAKES
12

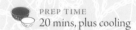 PREP TIME
20 mins, plus cooling

 COOK TIME
10–12 mins

Ingredients

450 g/1 lb plain flour,
plus extra for dusting

½ tsp salt

2 tsp baking powder

55 g/2 oz butter

2 tbsp caster sugar

250 ml/9 fl oz milk

3 tbsp milk, for glazing

strawberry jam and clotted
cream, to serve

Method

1 Preheat the oven to 220°C/425°F/
Gas Mark 7. Lightly flour or line a
baking sheet with baking paper.

2 Sift the flour, salt and baking powder
into a bowl. Rub in the butter until
the mixture resembles breadcrumbs.
Stir in the sugar. Make a well in the
centre and pour in the milk. Stir in

using a round-bladed knife and make
a soft dough.

3 Turn the mixture onto a floured
surface and lightly flatten the
dough until it is of an even thickness,
about 1 cm/½ inch. Don't be heavy
handed, scones need a light touch.

4 Use a 6-cm/2½-inch pastry cutter to
cut out the scones and place on the
prepared baking sheet. Glaze with a
little milk and bake in the preheated
oven for 10–12 minutes, until golden
and well risen. Cool on a wire rack and
serve freshly baked, with strawberry
jam and clotted cream.

2

2

4

The Afternoon Tea Party:

Throwing an afternoon tea party needn't be expensive. Mismatched china creates a lovely, vintage effect and it's worth scouring car boot sales, auctions, charity shops and (with permission) your grandmother's attic for treasure. Save pretty jars to fill with flowers, decant loose tea into containers and provide little finger bowls with slices of lemon and flower petals. Remember to arrange forks on the left, spoons and knives on the right.

Perhaps follow a theme. A bridal shower, for example, could feature delicate macaroons, champagne cocktails and a fragrant variety of tea. Or your theme could be as simple as drawing the curtains, lighting a fire and buttering crumpets in winter, arranging a vase of English garden flowers and a lace tablecloth in high summer or creating a West Country cream tea with scones, pots of clotted cream and home-made jam.

Tea Cakes

MAKES
10–12

PREP TIME
25 mins, plus resting

COOK TIME
18–20 mins

Ingredients

300 ml/10 fl oz pint milk

4 tsp dried yeast

55 g/2 oz caster sugar

450 g/1 lb strong plain flour,
plus extra for dusting

1 tsp salt

1 tsp ground mixed spice

115 g/4 oz currants

25 g/1 oz mixed peel, chopped

55 g/2 oz butter, melted,
plus extra for greasing

1 egg, beaten

sugar glaze made from 2 tbsp
sugar and 2 tbsp warm milk

Method

1 Warm the milk in a saucepan until just tepid and add the yeast with 1 teaspoon of the sugar. Mix well and allow to froth in a warm place for 15 minutes.

2 Sift the flour, salt and spice into a large mixing bowl and add the currants, peel and the remaining sugar. Make a well in the centre of the dry ingredients and pour in the milk mixture, the melted butter and egg.

Mix well using a wooden spoon at first and then by hand. Turn out onto a lightly floured surface and knead lightly until the dough is smooth and elastic.

3 Put the dough back into the bowl, cover with cling film and leave to rise in a warm place for 40–45 minutes until it has doubled in size. Knead the dough again lightly and divide into 10–12 even-sized buns, shaping well.

4 Preheat the oven to 220°C/425°F/ Gas Mark 7. Place the buns on two greased baking trays, cover with a damp tea towel and allow to rise again for 30–40 minutes. Bake the tea cakes in the oven for 18–20 minutes until they are golden brown. Remove from the oven, place on a wire rack and glaze with the sugar glaze while still hot.

2
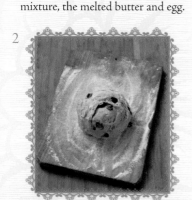

3

4

Vanilla Macaroons

 MAKES
16

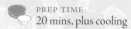 **PREP TIME**
20 mins, plus cooling

 COOK TIME
10–15 mins

Ingredients

75 g/2¾ oz ground almonds

115 g/4 oz icing sugar

2 large egg whites

50 g/1¾ oz caster sugar

½ tsp vanilla extract

FILLING

55 g/2 oz unsalted butter, softened

½ tsp vanilla extract

115 g/4 oz icing sugar, sifted

Method

1 Place the ground almonds and icing sugar in a food processor and process for 15 seconds. Sift the mixture into a bowl. Line two baking sheets with baking paper.

2 Place the egg whites in a clean, grease-free bowl and whisk until holding soft peaks. Gradually whisk in the caster sugar to make a firm, glossy meringue. Whisk in the vanilla extract.

3 Using a spatula, fold the almond mixture into the meringue one third at a time. When all the dry ingredients are thoroughly incorporated, continue to cut and fold the mixture until it forms a shiny batter.

4 Pour the mixture into a piping bag fitted with a 1-cm/½-inch plain nozzle. Pipe 32 small rounds onto the prepared baking sheets. Tap the baking sheets firmly onto a work surface to remove air bubbles. Leave at room temperature for 30 minutes. Preheat the oven to 160°C/325°F/Gas Mark 3.

5 Bake in the preheated oven for 10–15 minutes. Cool for 10 minutes, then carefully peel the macaroons off the baking paper. Leave to cool completely.

6 To make the filling, beat the butter and vanilla extract in a bowl until pale and fluffy. Gradually beat in the icing sugar until smooth and creamy. Use to sandwich pairs of macaroons together.

Cream Palmiers

 MAKES
8

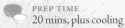 **PREP TIME**
20 mins, plus cooling

 COOK TIME
18–20 mins

Ingredients

40 g/1½ oz granulated sugar

225 g/8 oz ready-made puff pastry

400 ml/14 fl oz whipping cream or double cream

1 tbsp icing sugar, sifted

few drops vanilla extract

2 tbsp strawberry jam

Method

1 Preheat the oven to 220°C/425°F/ Gas Mark 7. Dust the work surface with half the sugar and roll the pastry out on the sugared work surface to a 25 x 30-cm/10 x 12-inch rectangle.

2 Sprinkle the rest of the sugar over the pastry and roll gently over it with the rolling pin. Roll the two short sides of the pastry into the centre until they

meet, moisten the edges that meet with a little water and press together gently. Cut across the roll into 16 even-sized slices.

3 Place the slices, cut side down, on a dampened baking tray. Use a rolling pin to flatten each one slightly.

4 Bake in the preheated oven for 15–18 minutes until crisp and golden brown, turning the palmiers over halfway through cooking. Transfer to a wire rack to cool.

5 Whip the cream, icing sugar and vanilla extract together until softly peaking. Sandwich the palmiers together with the jam and whipped cream.

Madeleines

MAKES	PREP TIME	COOK TIME
30	15 mins	10 mins

Ingredients

3 eggs

1 egg yolk

1 tsp vanilla extract

140 g/5 oz caster sugar

140 g/5 oz plain flour

1 tsp baking powder

140 g/5 oz unsalted butter, melted and cooled, plus extra for greasing

Method

1 Preheat the oven to 190°C/375°F/ Gas Mark 5. Lightly grease 30 holes in two to three standard-sized madeleine tins.

2 Place the eggs, egg yolk, vanilla extract and sugar in a large bowl and whisk with an electric handheld mixer until very pale and thick.

3 Sift in the flour and baking powder and fold in lightly and evenly using a metal spoon. Fold in the melted butter evenly.

4 Spoon the mixture into the prepared tins, filling to about three-quarters full. Bake in the preheated oven for 8–10 minutes, until risen and golden.

5 Remove the cakes carefully from the tins and cool on a wire rack. They are best served the day they are made.

Family Bakes

Family Bakes

There's nothing like the smell of a gorgeous cake baking in the oven to make you feel at home. While shop-bought cakes are perfectly proportioned and immaculately presented, nothing can compare to a slice of home-made cake served fresh from the oven.

From a classic chocolate cake to warm spiced apple-pie cupcakes, the recipes in this chapter all have an ability to soothe and satisfy in quantities large enough to meet the demands of family life.

Get children involved with the simpler recipes and plan ahead by baking in batches and freezing as soon as cakes have cooled to maintain maximum freshness.

Preheat your oven and weigh your ingredients in advance to get the best results. There are also a few keys items to invest in, it isn't necessary to buy everything at once but read your recipe through before you start to ensure you have the basics. Things you might find useful are:

Two shallow sandwich tins,
20–23 cm/8–9 inches

Deep square cake tin, 18 cm/7 inch

Ring tin, 24 cm/9 ½ inch

12-hole muffin and mini muffin tin

Muffin, cupcake and mini paper cases

Baking paper

Large mixing bowl

Large metal spoon

Wire rack

Small and large palette knives

Sieve

Electric handheld whisk

Large piping bag and large star nozzle

FOLLOW THE TIPS BELOW
TO GET PERFECT RESULTS:

Eggs should be at room temperature. Always beat first and then gradually add them to the creamed mixture. Beat well after each addition to avoid curdling.

As soon as you introduce air into cake mixture, whether in the form of sifted flour or whisked egg white, it is best to work gently, preserving as much air as possible. For best results use a large metal spoon.

Bake in the centre of the oven and don't be tempted to open the door too early – this can cause the cake to sink. To check if a sponge cake is ready, gently press the surface with your fingertips, it should be springy to the touch and not leave an impression. For deeper cakes, insert a skewer into the centre of the cake and it should come out clean.

Coffee & Walnut Cake

SERVES
8

PREP TIME
30 mins, plus cooling

COOK TIME
20–25 mins

Ingredients

175 g/6 oz unsalted butter,
softened, plus extra for greasing

175 g/6 oz light muscovado
sugar

3 large eggs, beaten

175 g/6 oz self-raising flour

1½ tsp baking powder

115 g/4 oz walnut pieces

3 tbsp strong black coffee
(cafetiere or instant made up
with hot water to taste)

walnut halves, to decorate

FROSTING

115 g/4 oz unsalted butter,
softened

200 g/7 oz icing sugar

1 tbsp strong black coffee

½ tsp vanilla extract

Method

1 Preheat the oven to 180°C/350°F/
Gas Mark 4. Grease two 20-cm/
8-inch sandwich tins and line with
baking paper.

2 Beat the butter and muscovado
sugar together until pale and creamy.
Gradually add the eggs, beating well
after each addition.

3 Sift the flour and baking powder into
the mixture, then fold in lightly and
evenly with a metal spoon. Fold in the
walnut pieces and the coffee. Divide
the mixture between the prepared cake
tins and smooth the surfaces. Bake in
the preheated oven for 20–25 minutes,
or until golden brown and springy to
the touch. Turn out onto a wire rack
to cool completely.

4 To make the frosting, beat together
the butter, icing sugar, coffee and
vanilla extract, mixing until smooth
and creamy.

5 Use about half the mixture to
sandwich the cakes together, then
spread the remaining frosting on
top and swirl with a palette knife.
Decorate with walnut halves.

Red Velvet Cake

SERVES
12

PREP TIME
20 mins, plus cooling

COOK TIME
25–30 mins

Ingredients

225 g/8 oz unsalted butter,
plus extra for greasing

4 tbsp water

55 g/2 oz cocoa powder

3 eggs, beaten

250 ml/9 fl oz buttermilk

2 tsp vanilla extract

2 tbsp red edible food colouring

280 g/10 oz plain flour

55 g/2 oz cornflour

1½ tsp baking powder

280 g/10 oz caster sugar

FROSTING

250 g/9 oz cream cheese

40 g/1½ oz unsalted butter

3 tbsp caster sugar

1 tsp vanilla extract

Method

1 Preheat the oven to 190°C/375°F/
Gas Mark 5. Grease two 23-cm/
9-inch sandwich tins and line with
baking paper.

2 Place the butter, water and cocoa
powder in a small saucepan and heat
gently, without boiling, stirring until
melted and smooth. Remove from the
heat and leave to cool slightly.

3 Beat together the eggs, buttermilk,
vanilla extract and food colouring in
a bowl. Beat in the butter mixture.
Sift together the flour, cornflour and
baking powder, then stir into the
mixture with the caster sugar.

4 Divide the mixture between the
prepared tins and bake in the
preheated oven for 25–30 minutes,

or until risen and firm to the touch.
Leave to cool in the tins for
3–4 minutes, then turn out onto a
wire rack to cool completely.

5 To make the frosting, beat together
all the ingredients until smooth. Use
about half of the frosting to sandwich
the cakes together, then spread the
remainder over the top.

Pineapple & Coconut Ring Cake

SERVES
12

PREP TIME
30 mins, plus cooling

COOK TIME
25 mins

Ingredients

432 g/15½ oz canned pineapple rings, drained

115 g/4 oz unsalted butter, softened, plus extra for greasing

175 g/6 oz caster sugar

2 eggs and 1 egg yolk, beaten

225 g/8 oz plain flour, plus extra for dusting

1 tsp baking powder

½ tsp bicarbonate of soda

40 g/1½ oz desiccated coconut

FROSTING

175 g/6 oz cream cheese

175 g/6 oz icing sugar

Method

1 Preheat the oven to 180°C/350°F/ Gas Mark 4. Grease and lightly flour a 24-cm/9½-inch ring tin. Place the pineapple rings in a blender or food processor and process briefly until just crushed.

2 Beat together the butter and caster sugar until light and fluffy. Gradually beat in the eggs until combined. Sift together the flour, baking powder and bicarbonate of soda over the egg mixture and fold in. Then fold in the crushed pineapple and the coconut.

3 Spoon the mixture into the prepared tin and bake in the preheated oven for 25 minutes, or until a skewer inserted into the centre comes out clean.

4 Allow to cool in the tin for 10 minutes before turning out onto a wire rack to cool completely. To make the frosting, mix together the cream cheese and icing sugar and spread over the cooled cake.

Classic Chocolate Cake

🧁 **SERVES**
10

🍮 **PREP TIME**
40 mins, plus chilling

🧤 **COOK TIME**
25–30 mins

Ingredients

55 g/2 oz cocoa powder

7 tbsp boiling water

200 g/7 oz butter, softened,
plus extra for greasing

125 g/4½ oz caster sugar

70 g/2½ oz soft light
brown sugar

4 eggs, beaten

1 tsp vanilla extract

200 g/7 oz self-raising flour

FROSTING

200 g/7 oz plain chocolate,
broken into pieces

115 g/4 oz unsalted butter

100 ml/3½ fl oz double cream

Method

1 Preheat the oven to 180°C/350°F/
Gas Mark 4. Grease two 20-cm/
8-inch sandwich tins and line with
baking paper.

2 Blend the cocoa powder and water to
a smooth paste and set aside. Put the
butter, caster sugar and brown sugar
into a large bowl and beat together
until pale and creamy. Gradually beat
in the eggs, then stir in the cocoa paste
and vanilla extract.

3 Sift in the flour and fold in gently.
Divide the mixture between
the prepared tins. Bake in the
preheated oven for 25–30 minutes,
or until risen and just springy to the
touch. Leave to cool in the tins
for 5 minutes, then turn out onto a
wire rack to cool completely.

4 To make the frosting, put the
chocolate and butter into a heatproof
bowl set over a saucepan of simmering

water, making sure the bowl doesn't
come in contact with the water, and
heat until melted. Remove from the
heat and stir in the cream. Leave to
cool for 20 minutes, then chill in
the refrigerator for 40–50 minutes,
stirring occasionally, until thick
enough to spread. Sandwich the
sponges togetherwith one third of the
frosting, then spread the remainder
over the top and sides of the cake.

Vanilla Frosted Cupcakes

🧁 **MAKES**
12

🥣 **PREP TIME**
15 mins, plus cooling

🧤 **COOK TIME**
15–20 mins

Ingredients

115 g/4 oz unsalted butter, softened

115 g/4 oz golden caster sugar

2 eggs, lightly beaten

115 g/4 oz self-raising flour

1 tbsp milk

crystallized rose petals, to decorate

FROSTING

175 g/6 oz unsalted butter, softened

2 tsp vanilla extract

2 tbsp milk

300 g/10½ oz icing sugar, sifted

Method

1 Preheat the oven to 180°C/350°F/ Gas Mark 4. Line a 12-hole muffin tin with paper cases.

2 Place the butter and sugar in a bowl and beat together until light and fluffy. Gradually beat in the eggs. Sift in the flour and fold in gently using a metal spoon. Fold in the milk.

3 Spoon the mixture into the paper cases. Bake in the preheated oven for 15–20 minutes until golden brown and firm to the touch. Transfer to a cooling rack and leave to cool.

4 To make the frosting, put the butter, vanilla extract and milk in a large bowl. Using an electric handheld whisk beat the mixture until smooth. Gradually beat in the icing sugar and continue beating for 2–3 minutes until the frosting is very light and creamy.

5 Spoon the frosting into a large piping bag fitted with a large star nozzle and pipe swirls of the frosting onto the top of each cupcake. Decorate each cupcake with crystallized rose petals.

2

2

4

Molten Chocolate Cupcakes

🧁 MAKES
9

🥣 PREP TIME
15 mins, plus cooling

🧤 COOK TIME
20 mins

Ingredients

175 g/6 oz soft margarine
175 g/6 oz caster sugar
3 large eggs

250 g/9 oz self-raising flour
3 tbsp cocoa powder

175 g/6 oz plain chocolate
icing sugar, for dusting

Method

1 Preheat the oven to 190°C/375°F/
Gas Mark 5. Put 9 paper baking cases
in two muffin tins.

2 Put the margarine, caster sugar, eggs,
flour and cocoa powder in a large bowl
and, using an electric handheld whisk,
beat together until just smooth.

3 Spoon half of the mixture into the
paper cases. Using a teaspoon, make
an indentation in the centre of each
cake. Break the chocolate evenly into
9 squares and place a piece on top
of each indentation, then spoon the
remaining cake mixture on top.

4 Bake the cupcakes in the preheated
oven for 20 minutes, or until well
risen and springy to the touch.
Leave the cupcakes to cool for
2–3 minutes before serving warm,
dusted with sifted icing sugar.

1

2

3

The Perfect Presentation

When you've put time into baking delicious cakes and treats for a family get-together it's always worthwhile thinking about the presentation. A beautiful china cake stand is a good investment. Use it for large family cakes, like the Rich Fruit Cake or Coffee and Walnut Cake, and it instantly adds elegance. It can also be used for mini cakes or cupcakes. Make sure that you don't position the cakes too close together or when one is removed the others could be damaged or topple off.

Alternatively for cupcakes, use a cupcake stand. These are available in kitchen supply stores and are ideal for displaying and serving lots of cupcakes. Also available are disposable cardboard stands, these come in a variety of colours and patterns and are often a cheaper solution. In addition to this think about pretty tea plates for people to put their cake on and colourful paper napkins.

You could also add cake flags to your cakes or bakes to highlight the occasion or indicate the flavour.

You can buy these ready-made, often themed for seasonal events, or make your own. To make your own, photocopy the designs on the opposite page or cut out a small piece of thin card or paper and use them as a template. Fold around a cocktail stick and glue the two halves together. For the heart-shaped ones, cut two identical shapes and stick them back-to-back on a cocktail stick. Try using different colours and patterns to match your theme.

Congratulations

Congratulations

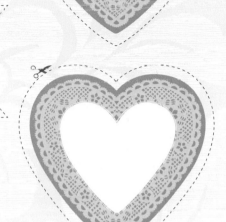

EAT ME!

EAT ME!

Warm Spiced Apple Pie Cupcakes

🧁 MAKES
12

🍮 PREP TIME
20 mins, plus cooling

🧤 COOK TIME
30 mins

Ingredients

50 g/1¾ oz butter, softened

70 g/2½ oz demerara sugar

1 egg, lightly beaten

150 g/5½ oz plain flour

1½ tsp baking powder

½ tsp ground mixed spice

1 large cooking apple, peeled, cored and finely chopped

1 tbsp orange juice

TOPPING

40 g/1½ oz plain flour

½ tsp ground mixed spice

25 g/1 oz butter

40 g/1½ oz caster sugar

Method

1 Preheat the oven to 180°C/350°F/ Gas Mark 4. Line a 12-hole muffin tin with 12 paper cases.

2 To make the topping, place the flour, mixed spice, butter and sugar in a large bowl and rub in with your fingertips until the mixture resembles fine breadcrumbs. Set aside.

3 To make the cupcakes, place the butter and sugar in a large bowl and beat together until light and fluffy, then gradually beat in the egg. Sift in the flour, baking powder and mixed spice and fold into the mixture, then fold in the chopped apple and orange juice. Spoon the mixture into the paper cases. Add the topping to cover the top of each cupcake and press down gently.

4 Bake in the preheated oven for 30 minutes, or until golden brown. Leave the cupcakes to cool in the tin for 2–3 minutes and serve warm, or leave to cool for 10 minutes and then transfer to a wire rack to cool completely.

48

Mini Chocolate Muffins

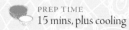

MAKES 12   **PREP TIME** 15 mins, plus cooling   **COOK TIME** 25 mins

Ingredients

15 g/½ oz cocoa powder

70 g/2½ oz self-raising flour

¼ tsp baking powder

25 g/1 oz light muscovado sugar

85 g/3 oz milk chocolate, roughly chopped

1 egg

3 tbsp milk

40 g/1½ oz lightly salted butter, melted

40 g/1½ oz plain chocolate, roughly chopped

Method

1 Preheat the oven to 190°C/375°F/ Gas Mark 5. Line a 12-hole mini muffin tin with 3-cm/1¼-inch mini paper cases.

2 Sift the cocoa powder, flour and baking powder into a mixing bowl. Stir in the light muscovado sugar and milk chocolate. In a separate mixing bowl, beat together the egg,

milk and butter with a fork until they are evenly combined. Tip the egg mixture into the flour. Gently fold the ingredients together until only just mixed.

3 Spoon the mixture into the paper cases. Bake in the preheated oven for 15 minutes, or until risen and just firm to the touch. Leave the muffins in the

tin for 2 minutes, then transfer them in their cases to a wire rack to cool.

4 Put the plain chocolate in a heatproof bowl set over a saucepan of simmering water, making sure the bowl doesn't come in contact with the water, and heat until melted. Using a teaspoon, drizzle the melted chocolate over the muffins and serve.

Raspberry Crumble Muffins

 MAKES
12

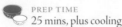 **PREP TIME**
25 mins, plus cooling

 COOK TIME
20 mins

Ingredients

280 g/10 oz plain flour
1 tbsp baking powder
½ tsp bicarbonate of soda
pinch of salt
115 g/4 oz caster sugar
2 eggs

250 ml/9 fl oz natural yogurt
85 g/3 oz butter, melted and
cooled
1 tsp vanilla extract
150 g/5½ oz frozen raspberries

CRUMBLE TOPPING
50 g/1¾ oz plain flour
35 g/1¼ oz butter
25 g/1 oz caster sugar

Method

1 Preheat the oven to 200°C/400°F/
Gas Mark 6. Line a 12-hole muffin
tin with paper cases.

2 To make the crumble topping, sift the
flour into a bowl. Cut the butter into
small pieces, add to the bowl with the
flour and rub it in with your fingertips
until the mixture resembles fine
breadcrumbs. Stir in the sugar and
set aside.

3 To make the muffins, sift together the
flour, baking powder, bicarbonate of
soda and salt into a large bowl. Stir in
the sugar.

4 Lightly beat the eggs in a large
bowl then beat in the yogurt, butter
and vanilla extract. Make a well in the
centre of the dry ingredients, pour in

the beaten liquid ingredients and add
the raspberries. Stir gently until just
combined; do not over-mix.

5 Spoon the mixture into the prepared
muffin tin. Scatter the crumble
topping over each muffin and press
down lightly. Bake in the preheated
oven for about 20 minutes until well
risen, golden brown and firm to
the touch.

6 Leave the muffins in the tin to cool
for 5 minutes then serve warm or
transfer to a wire rack and leave
to cool.

Pear & Chocolate Squares

MAKES	PREP TIME	COOK TIME
16	20 mins, plus cooling	1 hour 20 mins

Ingredients

140 g/5 oz wholemeal plain flour

140 g/5 oz self-raising flour

175 g/6 oz butter, diced, plus extra for greasing

100 g/3½ oz ground almonds

85 g/3 oz caster sugar

450 g/1 lb firm ripe pears, peeled, cored and roughly chopped

2 large eggs

25 g/1 oz cocoa powder

2 tsp baking powder

175 g/6 oz soft dark brown sugar

5 tbsp milk

Method

1 Preheat the oven to 180°C/350°F/ Gas Mark 4. Grease and line the base of an 18-cm/7-inch square deep cake tin. Sift the wholemeal and self-raising flours into a bowl. Add the butter and rub in with your fingertips until the mixture resembles fine breadcrumbs.

2 Transfer 25 g/1 oz of the mixture to a separate bowl. Add the ground almonds, caster sugar, pears and the white of one egg to the remaining mixture. Mix well.

3 Sift the cocoa powder and baking powder together. Stir into the remaining butter mixture with the brown sugar. Add the egg white, remaining egg yolks and milk. Mix well.

4 Spread half the chocolate mixture over the base of the prepared cake tin. Spread the pear mixture over the top. Cover with the remaining chocolate mixture and smooth the surface. Bake in the preheated oven for 1 hour, 10 minutes–1 hour, 20 minutes or until risen and the centre is firm to the touch. Leave to cool in the tin then turn out and cut into 16 squares.

1

3

4

Chocolate Brownies

MAKES
25

PREP TIME
15 mins, plus cooling

COOK TIME
18–20 mins

Ingredients

115 g/4 oz lightly salted butter, cut into pieces, plus extra for greasing

100 g/3½ oz plain chocolate, roughly chopped

2 eggs

175 g/6 oz light muscovado sugar

2 tsp vanilla extract

55 g/2 oz plain flour

25 g/1 oz cocoa powder

40 g/1½ oz pecan or walnuts, roughly chopped

Method

1 Preheat the oven to 200°C/400°F/ Gas Mark 6. Grease and line an 18-cm/7-inch shallow, square cake tin.

2 Put the butter and chocolate in a heatproof bowl, set the bowl over a saucepan of gently simmering water and heat until melted. Leave the mixture to cool slightly.

3 Put the eggs, sugar and vanilla in a mixing bowl and beat together with an electric handheld whisk until the mixture begins to turn frothy. Stir in the chocolate mixture until combined.

4 Sift the flour and cocoa powder into the bowl and scatter in the nuts. Stir together gently, then turn the mixture into the tin and level the surface.

5 Bake in the preheated oven for 18–20 minutes, or until the crust feels dry but gives a little when gently pressed. (If you're unsure, it's better to slightly under-cook brownies as they lose their gooeyness when they are over-baked.) Leave in the tin for 10 minutes, then transfer to a wire rack to cool. Cut the cake into 25 squares.

Beautiful Biscuits

Biscuits

A batch of biscuits, fresh from the oven is perhaps the surest way of enticing company into your kitchen (solitary cooks, be warned). They are also one of the quickest forms of baking, so ideal for busy families with lots of hungry mouths or for that moment when you just want something butterly sweet, and utterly comforting.

In one swift movement – taking into account some melting, mixing and a quick blast in the oven – you have dozens of crisp and chewy treats perfect for friends and family. A fail-safe option for bake sales and parties, they can also be stored in a jar to keep you going through the week.

The key items to invest in are a number of solid, flat metal baking trays that will fit in your oven with space all around for hot air to circulate. Here's a short summary of the other equipment you will need:

Two or three metal baking trays
Baking paper
Circular biscuit cutter
Piping bag
Large star nozzle
Wire cooling racks
Rolling pin
Sharp serrated knife

There are a few tips you can follow to make sure your biscuits turn out perfectly every time:

❦ Ensure you have read the recipe through before starting and don't skip any stages – if the recipe asks for you to chill the dough, this is because it makes the dough easier to cut.

❦ Preheat the oven to the correct temperature.

❦ Do any chopping, slicing or grating of ingredients before you start mixing them.

❦ When baking drop biscuits, make sure you space them well apart on the baking sheets to allow for expansion.

❦ Bake in the centre of the oven and if you have two trays swap them round halfway through the cooking time so the biscuits bake evenly.

❦ Freshly-baked biscuits are very soft when they first come out the oven, leave to cool slightly on the baking sheet before transferring to a wire rack to cool completely.

❦ Never store biscuits in a tin with cake, because they will lose their crispness. Instead, store in a separate airtight container.

Mini Florentines

🧁 MAKES
40

🥄 PREP TIME
30 mins, plus cooling

🧤 COOK TIME
20 mins

Ingredients

6 tbsp butter, plus extra
for greasing
flour, for dusting
75 g/2¾ oz caster sugar

2 tbsp sultanas or raisins
2 tbsp chopped glacé cherries
2 tbsp chopped stem ginger
25 g/1 oz sunflower seeds

100 g/3½ oz flaked almonds
2 tbsp double cream
175 g/6 oz plain or milk
chocolate, broken into pieces

Method

1 Preheat the oven to 180°C/350°F/
Gas Mark 4. Grease and flour
two baking trays or line with
greaseproof paper.

2 Place the butter in a small saucepan
and heat gently until melted. Add
the sugar, stir until dissolved, then
bring the mixture to the boil. Remove
from the heat and stir in the sultanas,
cherries, ginger, sunflower seeds and
almonds. Mix well, then beat in
the cream.

3 Place small teaspoons of the fruit
and nut mixture on to the prepared
baking trays, allowing plenty of room
for the mixture to spread during

baking. Bake in the preheated oven
for 10–12 minutes, or until light
golden in colour.

4 Remove from the oven and, while still
hot, use a circular biscuit cutter to pull
in the edges to form perfect circles.
Leave to cool and go crisp before
removing from the baking trays.

5 Put the chocolate in a heatproof bowl
set over a saucepan of simmering
water, making sure the bowl doesn't
come in contact with the water, and
heat until melted. Spread most of the
chocolate on to a sheet of greaseproof
paper. When the chocolate is on the
point of setting, place the biscuits
flat-side down on the chocolate and let
it harden completely.

6 Cut around the florentines and
remove from the greaseproof paper.
Spread a little more chocolate on the
coated side of the florentines and use
a fork to mark waves in the chocolate.
Leave to set. Keep cool.

Melting Moments

MAKES
32

PREP TIME
15 mins

COOK TIME
15–20 mins

Ingredients

350 g/12 oz unsalted butter, softened

85 g/3 oz icing sugar

½ tsp vanilla extract

300 g/10½ oz plain flour

50 g/1¾ oz cornflour

Method

1 Preheat the oven to 180°C/350°F/ Gas Mark 4. Line two large baking sheets with baking paper.

2 Place the butter and icing sugar in a large bowl and beat together until light and fluffy, then beat in the vanilla extract. Sift in the flour and cornflour and mix thoroughly.

3 Spoon the mixture into a piping bag fitted with a large star nozzle and pipe biscuits onto the prepared baking sheets, spaced well apart.

4 Bake in the preheated oven for 15–20 minutes, or until golden brown. Leave to cool on the baking sheets.

Viennese Fingers

 MAKES
16

 PREP TIME
20 mins, plus cooling

 COOK TIME
20 mins

Ingredients

100 g/3½ oz unsalted butter,
plus extra for greasing

25 g/1 oz golden caster sugar
½ tsp vanilla extract

100 g/3½ oz self-raising flour
100 g/3½ oz plain chocolate

Method

1 Preheat the oven to 160°C/325°F/
Gas Mark 3. Lightly grease two
baking sheets.

2 Place the butter, sugar and vanilla
extract in a bowl and cream together
until pale and fluffy. Stir in the flour,
mixing evenly to a fairly stiff dough.

3 Place the mixture in a piping bag
fitted with a large star nozzle and pipe
about 16 fingers, each 6 cm/2½ inches
long, onto the prepared baking sheets
spaced well apart.

4 Bake in the preheated oven for
10–15 minutes, until golden brown.
Leave to cool on the baking sheets
for a few minutes, then transfer
the biscuits to wire racks to cool
completely.

5 Place the chocolate in a small heatproof
bowl set over a saucepan of simmering
water, making sure the bowl doesn't
come in contact with the water, and
heat until melted. Remove from the
heat. Dip the ends of each biscuit into
the chocolate and leave to set.

Black & White Biscuits

MAKES
20

PREP TIME
20 mins, plus chilling

COOK TIME
20 mins

Ingredients

115 g/4 oz unsalted butter, softened, plus extra for greasing

1 tsp vanilla extract

175 g/6 oz caster sugar

2 eggs, beaten

300 g/10½ oz plain flour

½ tsp baking powder

200 ml/7 fl oz milk

ICING

225 g/8 oz icing sugar

125 ml/4 fl oz double cream

⅛ tsp vanilla extract

75 g/2¾ oz plain chocolate, broken into pieces

Method

1 Preheat the oven to 190°C/375°F/ Gas Mark 5. Grease three baking sheets. Place the butter, vanilla extract and caster sugar in a large bowl. Beat the mixture with a whisk until light and fluffy and then beat in the eggs one at a time.

2 Sift the flour and baking powder and fold into the creamed mixture, loosening with milk as you go until both are used up and the mix is of dropping consistency. Drop heaped tablespoonfuls of the mixture, spaced well apart, on the prepared baking sheets. Place in the preheated oven and bake for 15 minutes, or until turning golden at the edges and light to the touch. Transfer to wire racks to cool completely.

3 To make the icing, put the icing sugar in a bowl and mix in half the cream and the vanilla extract. The consistency should be thick but spreadable. Using a palette knife, spread half of each biscuit with white icing. Now, place the chocolate in a bowl set over a saucepan of simmering water, making sure the bowl doesn't come in contact with the water, and heat until melted. Remove from the heat and stir in the remaining cream. Spread the dark icing over the uncoated biscuit halves.

1

2

3

Pistachio & Almond Juiles

MAKES
6

PREP TIME
30 mins, plus cooling

COOK TIME
10–15 mins

Ingredients

1 egg white
55 g/2 oz golden caster sugar
25 g/1 oz plain flour

25 g/1 oz pistachio nuts,
finely chopped
25 g/1 oz ground almonds

½ tsp almond extract
40 g/1½ oz unsalted butter,
melted and cooled

Method

1 Preheat the oven to 160°C/325°F/
Gas Mark 3. Line two baking trays
with baking paper.

2 Whisk the egg white lightly with the
sugar, then stir in the flour, pistachios,
ground almonds, almond extract and
butter, mixing to a soft paste.

3 Place walnut-sized spoonfuls of the
mixture on the prepared baking trays
and use the back of the spoon to
spread as thinly as possible.
Bake in the preheated oven for
10–15 minutes, until pale golden.

4 Quickly lift each biscuit with a
palette knife and place over the side
of a rolling pin to shape into a curve.
When set, transfer to a wire rack
to cool.

Orange & Lemon Biscuits

MAKES
30

PREP TIME
30 mins, plus chilling

COOK TIME
10–15 mins

Ingredients

225 g/8 oz butter, softened

140 g/5 oz caster sugar

1 egg yolk, lightly beaten

280 g/10 oz plain flour

finely grated rind of 1 orange

finely grated rind of 1 lemon

salt

TO DECORATE

1 tbsp lightly beaten egg white

1 tbsp lemon juice

115 g/4 oz icing sugar

few drops yellow food colouring

few drops orange food colouring

about 15 lemon jelly slices

about 15 orange jelly slices

Method

1 Put the butter and sugar into a bowl and mix well with a wooden spoon, then beat in the egg yolk. Sift together the flour and a pinch of salt into the mixture and stir until thoroughly combined. Halve the dough and gently knead the orange rind into one half and the lemon rind into the other. Shape into balls, wrap in clingfilm and chill in the refrigerator for 30–60 minutes.

2 Preheat the oven to 190°C/375°F/ Gas Mark 5. Line two baking sheets with baking paper.

3 Unwrap the orange-flavoured dough and roll out between two sheets of baking paper. Stamp out rounds with a 6-cm/2½-inch cutter and put them on a prepared baking sheet spaced well apart. Repeat with the lemon-flavoured dough and stamp out crescents. Put them on the other prepared baking sheet spaced well apart.

4 Bake for 10–15 minutes, until golden brown. Leave to cool for 5–10 minutes, then carefully transfer to wire racks to cool completely.

5 To decorate, mix together the egg white and lemon juice. Gradually beat in the icing sugar with a wooden spoon until smooth. Spoon half the icing into another bowl. Stir yellow food colouring into one bowl and orange into the other. Leave the biscuits on the racks. Spread the icing over the biscuits and decorate with the jelly slices. Leave to set.

Blueberry & Orange Biscuits

MAKES
30

PREP TIME
25 mins, plus chilling

COOK TIME
10–15 mins

Ingredients

225 g/8 oz butter, softened
140 g/5 oz caster sugar
1 egg yolk, lightly beaten
1 tsp orange extract

280 g/10 oz plain flour
100 g/3½ oz dried blueberries
100 g/3½ oz cream cheese
grated rind of 1 orange

40 g/1½ oz macadamia nuts, finely chopped
salt

Method

1 Put the butter and sugar into a bowl and mix well with a wooden spoon, then beat in the egg yolk and orange extract. Sift the flour and a pinch of salt into the mixture, add the blueberries and stir until thoroughly combined. Shape the dough into a log, wrap in clingfilm and chill in the refrigerator for 30–60 minutes.

2 Preheat the oven to 190°C/375°F/Gas Mark 5. Line two baking sheets with baking paper.

3 Unwrap the dough and cut into 5-mm/¼-inch slices with a sharp serrated knife. Put them on the prepared baking sheets, spaced well apart.

4 Bake for 10–15 minutes, until golden brown. Leave to cool on the baking sheets for 5–10 minutes, then using a palette knife, carefully transfer to wire racks to cool completely.

5 Just before serving, beat the cream cheese in a bowl and stir in the orange rind. Spread the mixture over the biscuits and sprinkle with the chopped nuts.

Pastry Cream Biscuits

MAKES
15

PREP TIME
30 mins, plus chilling

COOK TIME
20 mins

Ingredients

225 g/8 oz butter, softened

140 g/5 oz caster sugar, plus extra for decoration

1 egg, separated

2 tsp vanilla extract

280 g/10 oz plain flour

pinch of salt

15 small bunches of redcurrants

225 g/8 oz icing sugar, sifted

¼ tsp lemon extract

PASTRY CREAM

2 egg yolks, lightly beaten

4 tbsp caster sugar

1 tbsp cornflour

1 heaped tbsp plain flour

300 ml/10 fl oz milk

few drops of vanilla extract

1 egg white

Method

1 Place the butter and sugar in a large bowl and beat together. Lightly beat the egg yolk and then beat into the mixture with the vanilla extract. Sift in the flour and salt and stir until thoroughly combined. Halve the dough, wrap in clingfilm and chill in the refrigerator for 45 minutes.

2 Preheat the oven to 190°C/ 375°F/ Gas Mark 5. Line two large baking sheets with baking paper. Roll out the dough between sheets of baking paper. Cut out 30 rounds with a 6-cm/ 2½-inch cookie cutter and place them on the baking sheets. Bake in the preheated oven for 12 minutes, or until golden brown. Leave to cool for 5 minutes, then transfer to wire racks to cool.

3 To make the pastry cream, beat the egg yolks and sugar together. Sift in the flours and beat well. Stir in 3 tablespoons of the milk and the vanilla extract. Bring the remaining milk to the boil, then whisk it into the mixture. Return to the pan and bring to the boil, stirring, then beat until cool.

4 Whisk the egg white until stiff. Spoon a little pastry cream into a bowl, fold in the egg white, then fold into the rest of the cream. Heat for 2 minutes, then leave to cool. Sandwich the biscuits together with the pastry cream.

5 Beat the egg white. Dip the redcurrants into the beaten egg white and roll in caster sugar. Mix the icing sugar, lemon extract and enough water to make a smooth icing. Spread the icing over the biscuits and decorate with the redcurrants.

Home-made Gifts

With the ever-growing trend of all things vintage, making your own gifts has never been more popular. Home-made biscuits make brilliant gifts – wrapped in cellophane and tied with a bow, they are sure to impress. Add a home-made gift tag and the home-made gift is complete! The gift tags on the opposite page can be photocopied and glued onto card.

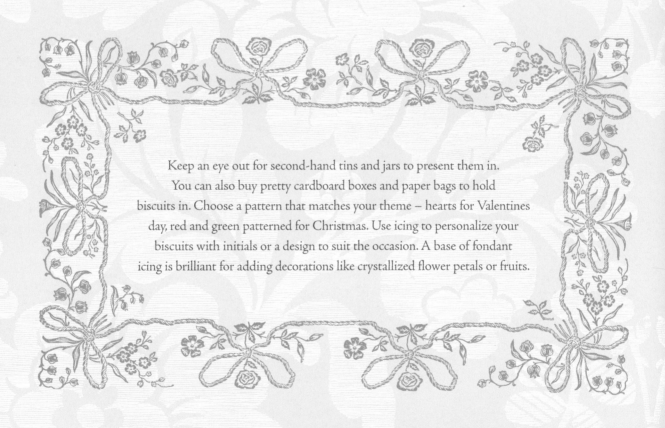

Keep an eye out for second-hand tins and jars to present them in. You can also buy pretty cardboard boxes and paper bags to hold biscuits in. Choose a pattern that matches your theme – hearts for Valentines day, red and green patterned for Christmas. Use icing to personalize your biscuits with initials or a design to suit the occasion. A base of fondant icing is brilliant for adding decorations like crystallized flower petals or fruits.

Baked with love by

....

Created with love by

....

Try these tasty

....

Date made

....

Ingredients

....

....

....

Created with love by

....

Created with love by

....

Baked with love by

....

Rose Water Biscuits

🧁 MAKES
60

🥣 PREP TIME
25 mins, plus chilling

🧤 COOK TIME
10–12 mins

Ingredients

225 g/8 oz butter, softened
225 g/8 oz caster sugar
1 large egg, lightly beaten
1 tbsp rose water

280 g/10 oz plain flour
1 tsp baking powder
pinch of salt

ICING
1 egg white
250 g/9 oz icing sugar
2 tsp plain flour
2 tsp rose water
few drops of pink food colouring

Method

1 Place the butter and sugar in a large bowl and beat together until light and fluffy, then beat in the egg and rose water. Sift together the flour, baking powder and salt into the mixture and stir until combined. Shape the dough into a log, wrap in clingfilm and chill in the refrigerator for 1–2 hours.

2 Preheat the oven to 190°C/ 375°F/ Gas Mark 5. Line two to three baking sheets with baking paper.

3 Unwrap the dough, cut into thin slices with a sharp serrated knife and place on the baking sheets, spaced well apart.

4 Bake in the preheated oven for 10–12 minutes, or until light golden brown. Leave to cool on the baking sheets for 10 minutes, then transfer the biscuits to wire racks to cool completely.

5 To make the icing, use a fork to lightly beat the egg white in a bowl. Sift in half the icing sugar and stir well, then sift in the remaining icing sugar and flour and mix in enough rose water to make a smooth, easy-to-spread icing. Stir in a few drops of pink food colouring.

6 Leave the biscuits on the racks.

Gently spread the icing over them and leave to set.

Chocolate Wreaths

 MAKES
16

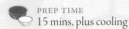 PREP TIME
15 mins, plus cooling

 COOK TIME
15–20 mins

Ingredients

125 g/4 ½ oz butter, softened,
plus extra for greasing

40 g/1 ½ oz icing sugar

125 g/4 ½ oz plain flour

25 g/1 oz cornflour

15 g/ ½ oz cocoa powder

½ tsp vanilla extract

ICING

100 g/3 ½ oz icing sugar

2 tsp cocoa powder

2 tbsp milk

Method

1 Preheat the oven to 180°C/350°F/
Gas Mark 4. Grease two
baking sheets.

2 Put the butter and icing sugar in a
bowl and beat together until pale and
creamy. Sift over the flour, cornflour
and cocoa powder and beat well until
smooth and creamy. Beat in the
vanilla extract.

3 Spoon the mixture into a large piping
bag fitted with a large star nozzle and
pipe 16 x 7-cm/2¾-inch diameter
circles on to the prepared baking
sheets.

4 Bake in the preheated oven for
15–20 minutes until just firm. Leave
to cool on the baking sheets for
5 minutes then transfer to a wire
rack to cool completely.

5 To make the icing, sift the icing
sugar and cocoa powder into a
bowl and beat in the milk to make
a smooth icing. Spoon the icing on top
of the biscuits.

2

3

5

Perfect Pastries & Pies

Perfect Pastries & Pies

It's incredible to think that the simple alchemy of pastry, made with flour, fat and water, has the power to revolutionize your home baking. Line a tin with a thin layer of sweet shortcrust pastry and any fruit or leftover dairy can quickly be transformed into a delicious pie or tart.

There are, of course, different types of pastry for different requirements. Choux pastry, as used in chocolate éclairs, is a thick cooked blend of flour and butter with eggs beaten through. Piped and baked, it results in light, airy pastry with a hollow centre cavity, perfect for filling with luscious pastry cream.

Puff pastry consists of thin layers, which billow into crisp airiness when baked, making it suitable for pastries such as apple turnovers and sweet puffs. The most versatile pastry in this chapter is, however, sweet shortcrust. Rolled thinly, it provides a crisp base for everything from summery fruit tarts to decadent Honey, Walnut & Ricotta Pies.

Useful equipment:
Baking tray
Large piping bag and plain nozzle
Pastry brush
12-hole muffin and mini muffin tin
Rolling pin
Plain and fluted biscuit cutter
Deep tartlet tins (preferably metal)
Baking paper
Baking beans

Cinnamon Swirls

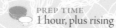

🧁 MAKES
12

🍮 PREP TIME
1 hour, plus rising

🧤 COOK TIME
20–30 mins

Ingredients

225 g/8 oz strong white flour

½ tsp salt

10 g/¼ oz easy-blend dried yeast

2 tbsp butter, cut into small pieces, plus extra for greasing

1 egg, lightly beaten

125 ml/4 fl oz lukewarm milk

2 tbsp maple syrup, for glazing

FILLING

4 tbsp butter, softened

2 tsp ground cinnamon

50 g/1¾ oz soft light brown sugar

50 g/1¾ oz currants

Method

1 Grease a baking sheet with a little butter.

2 Sift the flour and salt into a mixing bowl. Stir in the yeast. Rub in the butter with your fingertips until the mixture resembles breadcrumbs. Add the egg and milk and mix to form a dough.

3 Form the dough into a ball, place in a greased bowl, cover with clingfilm and leave to stand in a warm place for

about 40 minutes, or until doubled in size. Lightly knock back the dough for 1 minute, then roll out to a rectangle measuring 30 x 23 cm/12 x 9 inches.

4 To make the filling, cream together the butter, cinnamon and sugar until light and fluffy. Spread the filling evenly over the dough rectangle, leaving a 2.5-cm/1-inch border all around. Sprinkle the currants evenly over the top.

5 Roll up the dough from one of the long edges, and press down to seal. Cut the roll into 12 slices. Place them, cut-side down, on the baking sheet, cover and leave to stand for 30 minutes.

6 Meanwhile, preheat the oven to 190°C/375°F/Gas Mark 5. Bake the buns in the preheated oven for 20–30 minutes, or until well risen. Brush with the maple syrup and leave to cool slightly before serving.

Apple Turnovers

MAKES
8

PREP TIME
40 mins

COOK TIME
15–20 mins

Ingredients

250 g/9 oz ready-made
puff pastry

flour, for dusting

milk, for glazing

double cream, whipped, to serve

FILLING

450 g/1 lb cooking apples,
peeled, cored and chopped

grated rind of 1 lemon (optional)

pinch of ground cloves (optional)

3 tbsp sugar

ORANGE SUGAR

1 tbsp sugar, for sprinkling

finely grated rind of 1 orange

Method

1 To make the filling, mix together the apples, lemon rind and ground cloves, if using, but do not add the sugar yet as the juice will then seep out of the apples. For the orange sugar, mix together the sugar and orange rind.

2 Preheat the oven to 220°C/425°F/ Gas Mark 7. Roll out the pastry on a floured work surface into a 60 x 30-cm/24 x 12-inch rectangle. Cut the pastry in half lengthways, then across into four to make eight 15-cm/ 6-inch squares.

3 Mix the sugar into the apple filling. Brush each square lightly with milk and place a little of the apple filling in the centre. Fold over one corner diagonally to meet the opposite one, making a triangular turnover, and press the edges together very firmly. Place on a baking sheet. Repeat with the remaining squares. Brush with milk and sprinkle with the orange sugar. Bake in the preheated oven for 15–20 minutes, or until browned. Leave to cool on a wire rack. Serve with the double cream.

Chocolate Éclairs

🧁 **MAKES**
12

🍵 **PREP TIME**
45 mins, plus cooling

🧤 **COOK TIME**
45 mins

Ingredients

CHOUX PASTRY

150 ml/5 fl oz water

70 g/2½ oz butter, cut into small pieces, plus extra for greasing

100 g/3½ oz plain flour, sifted

2 eggs

PASTRY CREAM

2 eggs, lightly beaten

4 tbsp caster sugar

2 tbsp cornflour

300 ml/10 fl oz milk

½ tsp vanilla extract

ICING

2 tbsp butter

1 tbsp milk

1 tbsp cocoa powder

55 g/2 oz icing sugar

50 g/1¾ oz milk chocolate, broken into pieces

Method

1 Preheat the oven to 200°C/400°F/ Gas Mark 6. Lightly grease a baking sheet.

2 To make the choux pastry, place the water in a saucepan, add the butter and heat gently until the butter melts. Bring to a rolling boil, then remove the saucepan from the heat and add the flour all at once, beating well until the mixture leaves the sides of the saucepan and forms a ball. Leave to cool slightly, then gradually beat in the eggs to form a smooth, glossy mixture. Spoon into a large piping bag fitted with a 1-cm/½-inch plain nozzle.

3 Sprinkle the baking sheet with a little water. Pipe 12 éclairs 7.5 cm/3 inches long, spaced well apart. Bake for 30–35 minutes, or until crisp and golden. Make a small slit in the side of each éclair to let the steam escape. Leave to cool on a wire rack.

4 Meanwhile, make the pastry cream. Whisk the eggs and sugar until thick and creamy, then fold in the cornflour. Heat the milk until almost boiling and pour onto the eggs, whisking. Transfer to the saucepan and cook over a low heat, stirring until thick. Remove the saucepan from the heat and stir in the vanilla extract. Cover with baking paper and leave to cool.

5 To make the icing, melt the butter with the milk in a saucepan. Remove from the heat and stir in the cocoa and sugar. Split the éclairs lengthways and pipe in the pastry cream. Spread the icing over the top of the éclairs. Place a little milk chocolate in a heatproof bowl set over a saucepan of simmering water, making sure the bowl doesn't come in contact with the water, and heat until melted. Drizzle over the chocolate icing and leave to set. Serve immediately.

Caramelized Apple Tarts

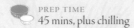

MAKES	PREP TIME	COOK TIME
12	45 mins, plus chilling	36 mins

Ingredients

450 g/1 lb ready-made sweet
shortcrust pastry, chilled

a little plain flour, for dusting

5 Granny Smith apples,
quartered, cored and peeled

85 g/3 oz caster sugar

finely grated rind and juice of
1 lemon

2 eggs

15 g/½ oz butter, plus extra for
greasing

3 tbsp icing sugar, sifted

Method

1 Lightly grease a 12-hole muffin tin. Roll the pastry out thinly on a lightly floured surface. Using a plain biscuit cutter, stamp out 12 circles, each 10 cm/4 inches in diameter. Press these gently into the prepared tin, rerolling the trimmings as needed. Prick the base of each with a fork, then chill in the refrigerator for 15 minutes. Preheat the oven to 190°C/375°F/Gas Mark 5. Line the pastry cases with squares of crumpled baking paper and baking beans. Bake in the preheated oven for 10 minutes.

Remove the paper and beans and cook the cases for 2–3 minutes more, or until the base of the pastry is crisp and dry. Turn the oven down to 180°C/350°F/Gas Mark 4.

2 Roughly grate eight of the apple quarters into a mixing bowl. Add two-thirds of the caster sugar, all the lemon rind and juice and the eggs and whisk together. Spoon the filling into the cases.

3 Thinly slice the remaining apples and arrange them overlapping on top of the pies. Sprinkle with the remaining caster sugar and then dot the pies with the butter. Bake in the preheated oven for 20–25 minutes, or until the filling is set.

4 Dust with the icing sugar and return the pies to the oven for 5 minutes, or until the sugar has caramelized pale gold. Leave to cool in the tins for 10 minutes, then transfer the tarts to a wire rack to cool. Serve warm or cold.

Blueberry Tarts

 MAKES
24

 PREP TIME
25 mins

 COOK TIME
18 mins

Ingredients

300 g/10½ oz blueberries

2 tsp cornflour

55 g/2 oz caster sugar

4 tsp water

55 g/2 oz plain flour, plus extra
for dusting

grated rind of 1 lemon

40 g/1½ oz butter, diced,
plus extra for greasing

325 g/11½ oz ready-made sweet
shortcrust pastry, chilled

Method

1 Preheat the oven to 190°C/375°F/
Gas Mark 5. Lightly grease
two x 12-hole mini muffin tins.

2 Put half the blueberries in a small
saucepan with the cornflour, half the
caster sugar and the water. Cook, over
a medium heat, stirring constantly,
for 2–3 minutes. Take the pan off

the heat and add the remaining
blueberries. For the streusel, put
the flour, lemon rind, butter and
remaining sugar in a bowl. Toss
together, then rub it through your
fingers and thumbs until it looks like
fine breadcrumbs.

3 Roll the pastry out thinly on a lightly
floured surface. Using a fluted cookie

cutter, stamp out 24 circles each
6 cm/2½ inches in diameter.
Press these into the prepared tins,
rerolling trimmings as needed.
Spoon the blueberry filling into the
cases, then sprinkle the tops of the
tarts with the streusel mixture. Bake
in the preheated oven for 15 minutes,
or until the topping is pale gold.

Summer Fruit Tartlets

 MAKES
12

 PREP TIME
25 mins, plus chilling

 COOK TIME
18 mins

Ingredients

200 g/7 oz plain flour, plus extra
for dusting

85 g/3 oz icing sugar, sifted

55 g/2 oz ground almonds

115 g/4 oz butter

1 egg yolk

1 tbsp milk

fresh summer berries, to decorate

FILLING

225 g/8 oz cream cheese

icing sugar, to taste, plus extra,
sifted, for dusting

Method

1 Sift the flour and icing sugar into a bowl. Stir in the almonds. Add the butter, rubbing in until the mixture resembles breadcrumbs. Add the egg yolk and milk and work in until the dough binds together. Wrap in clingfilm and chill for 30 minutes. Meanwhile, preheat the oven to 200°C/400°F/Gas Mark 6.

2 Roll out the dough on a lightly floured surface and use it to line 12 deep tartlet tins. Prick the bases and press a piece of foil into each.

3 Bake in the preheated oven for 10–15 minutes, or until light golden brown. Remove the foil and bake for a further 2–3 minutes. Transfer to a wire rack to cool.

4 To make the filling, place the cream cheese and icing sugar in a bowl and mix together. Place a spoonful of filling in each tartlet and arrange the berries on top.

5 Dust with sifted icing sugar and serve.

Salted Caramel Pies

MAKES
4

PREP TIME
30 mins, plus chilling

COOK TIME
10 mins

Ingredients

CRUMB CRUST

175 g/6 oz digestive biscuits,
finely crushed

85 g/3 oz butter, melted

FILLING

300 g/10½ oz caster sugar

150 g/5½ oz butter

¼ tsp sea salt crystals

125 ml/4 fl oz double cream

TOPPING

150 ml/5 fl oz double cream

chocolate curls or shavings

Method

1 To make the crumb crust, place
the crushed biscuits in a bowl and
stir in the melted butter. Divide the
mixture between four tartlet tins and
press down firmly into the base and
up the sides of each tin. Chill in the
refrigerator for 30 minutes.

2 To make the filling, place the sugar and
4 tablespoons of water into a heavy-
based saucepan. Heat gently, stirring,

until the sugar has dissolved. Bring
the syrup to a boil and boil, without
stirring, until the liquid is a golden
toffee colour. Remove from the heat
and cool for 2 minutes, then carefully
stir in the butter and half the salt.

3 Gradually whisk in the cream and
continue whisking until the mixture
is smooth and glossy. Transfer to a
heatproof bowl and leave to cool and

thicken, stirring occasionally. Stir in
the rest of the salt. Spoon the cooled
caramel into the tartlet cases.

4 For the topping, whip the cream
until holding soft peaks. Drop large
spoonfuls on top of the caramel filling,
scatter over the chocolate curls or
shavings and serve.

1

2

3

Pies for Parties

The trend towards baking individual or mini tarts is, let's face it, a great way of having your own cake and eating it all to yourself. Mini pies are easier to serve at parties, forgoing the headache of baking one massive cake and hoping everyone gets an equal slice. Simple decorations like chocolate curls, a little streusel topping, some icing or a dollop of pillowy whipped cream add a finishing touch to mini tarts. Or, if you really want to get your pâtissier's hat on, whip a piping bag out and go for it.

When it comes to serving your mini pastries, help guests and friends along by providing the right cutlery. Something creamy with a soft filling like a summer fruit or caramelized apple tart will require a cake fork. Pastries like apple turnovers or tart tatin are at their best warm, served on a side plate with a dollop of cream and a spoon, while a small puff or mini tart can be eaten with fingers, but be sure to provide napkins.

Toffee Chocolate Puffs

🧁 **MAKES**
12

🥧 **PREP TIME**
30 mins, plus chilling

🧤 **COOK TIME**
20–25 mins

Ingredients

375 g/13 oz ready-rolled
puff pastry

140 g/5 oz plain chocolate,
broken into pieces

300 ml/10 fl oz double cream

50 g/1¾ oz caster sugar

4 egg yolks

4 tbsp ready-made toffee sauce

whipped cream, to serve

cocoa powder, for dusting

Method

1 Line the base of a 12-hole muffin tin
with discs of baking paper. Cut out
12 x 5-cm/2-inch rounds from
the edge of the pastry and cut the
remainder into 12 strips. Roll the
strips to half their thickness and line
the sides of each hole with 1 strip.
Place a disc of pastry in each base and
press together to seal and make a tart
case. Prick the bases and chill in the
refrigerator for 30 minutes.

2 Preheat the oven to 200°C/400°F/
Gas Mark 6. While the pastry is
chilling, place the chocolate in a
heatproof bowl set over a saucepan
of simmering water, making sure the
bowl doesn't come in contact with the
water, and heat until melted. Leave to
cool slightly, then stir in the cream.

3 Place the sugar and egg yolks in a
bowl and beat together, then mix
well with the melted chocolate. Place

a teaspoonful of the toffee sauce
into each tart case, then divide the
chocolate mixture evenly between
the tarts. Bake in the preheated oven
for 20–25 minutes, turning the tin
around halfway through cooking,
until just set. Leave to cool in the
tin, then remove carefully and
serve with whipped cream, dusted
with cocoa.

1

2

3

Honey, Walnut & Ricotta Pies

MAKES 24

PREP TIME 45 mins, plus cooling

COOK TIME 25 mins

Ingredients

a little butter, for greasing

a little olive oil, for greasing

325 g/11½ oz ready-made sweet shortcrust pastry, chilled

a little plain flour, for dusting

125 g/4½ oz walnut pieces

225 g/8 oz ricotta cheese

2 egg yolks

5 tbsp runny orange blossom honey

a large pinch of ground cinnamon

115 g/4 oz granulated sugar

1 tbsp water

200 g/7 oz Greek yogurt, to serve

Method

1 Lightly grease 2 x 12-section mini muffin tins and oil a baking tray. Preheat the oven to 180°C/350°F/ Gas Mark 4.

2 Roll the pastry out thinly on a lightly floured surface. Using a fluted biscuit cutter, stamp out 24 circles each 6 cm/2½ inches in diameter. Press these gently into the prepared tins, rerolling the trimmings as needed.

3 Lightly toast half the walnut pieces in a dry non-stick frying pan. Leave them to cool, then roughly chop them.

4 Lightly whisk the ricotta, egg yolks, 4 tablespoons of the honey and the cinnamon together in a mixing bowl until just mixed. Stir in the toasted walnuts. Spoon the filling into the cases.

5 Bake in the preheated oven for 20 minutes, or until the filling is golden brown. Leave in the tin for 10 minutes to cool.

6 Meanwhile, for the praline put the sugar, remaining 1 tablespoon of honey and the water into the frying pan and heat gently without stirring until the sugar has dissolved. Tilt the pan to mix any remaining grains of sugar into the syrup. Add the remaining walnuts and cook over a medium heat, again without stirring, for about 5 minutes, or until the syrup turns a rich golden brown. Keep a watchful eye on the syrup as it will suddenly begin to change colour, darkening first around the edges.

Tilt the pan to mix if needed, then quickly pour the praline onto the prepared baking tray and leave to cool and harden.

7 Loosen the pies with a round-bladed knife and transfer them to a plate. Just before serving, top them with spoonfuls of yogurt. Loosen the praline from the baking tray with a knife, then break or cut it into thin shards and press pieces of it into the yogurt.

Tarte Tatin

🧁 SERVES
6

☕ PREP TIME
20 mins, plus resting

🧤 COOK TIME
45 mins

Ingredients

200 g/7 oz caster sugar
150 g/5½ oz unsalted butter

800 g/1 lb 12 oz Cox or Golden
Delicious apples

350 g/12 oz puff pastry

Method

1 Place a 20-cm/8-inch ovenproof frying pan over a low heat and add the sugar. Melt the sugar until it starts to caramelize, but do not let it burn, then add the butter and stir it in to make a light toffee sauce. Remove from the heat.

2 Peel the apples and cut them into eighths vertically. Core the apples and lay them in the pan on top of the toffee sauce, cut side up. They should fill the pan. If there are any large gaps, add a few more apple pieces. Put the pan over a medium heat and cover. Simmer, without stirring, for about 5–10 minutes until the apples have soaked up some of the sauce, then remove from the heat.

3 Preheat the oven to 190°C/375°F/ Gas Mark 5. Roll out the pastry so that it will thickly cover the pan, with extra overhanging the sides. Lay it on top of the apples and tuck the edges down inside between the fruit and the pan until it is sealed. Don't worry about making it look too neat – it will be turned over before serving.

4 Put the pan into the preheated oven and bake for 25–35 minutes, checking to make sure the pastry doesn't burn. The pastry should be puffed and golden. Remove from the oven and leave to rest for 30–60 minutes.

5 To serve, make sure the tart is still a little warm and place a plate on top of the frying pan. Carefully turn it over and lift the pan off. Serve warm.

Special Moments

Special Moments

For every high day and holiday, tradition provides there will be cake. Whether it's a stand of birthday cupcakes, each with a candle, wedding cake festooned in iced rosebuds or a plateful of Easter cookies, you can always tell the occasion from dessert.

When planning your party it's worth following a few simple rules: plan as far in advance as possible, preparing and freezing what food you can; consider the tastes of your guests; provide enough food, drink and chairs; ask for help if you need it and don't be afraid to exercise your imagination.

Party planning checklist:

* Draw up invitation list
* Choose theme: make, borrow or buy decorations and props
* Send invitations
* Design menu: plan what can be made in advance and write a shopping list
* Clean and prepare linen and cutlery
* Plan what dishes you will need: source whatever you don't have
* Decorate for the occasion
* Buy and arrange flowers: decorate the house the day before
* On the day: arrange chairs, lay the table, and make last minute touches to food

Photocopy this invitation and send out to your guests.

Invitation

Dear ....

You have been invited to ....

....

By ....

On ....

At ....

RSVP by ....

Summer Garden Cupcakes

 MAKES
8

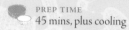 **PREP TIME**
45 mins, plus cooling

 COOK TIME
15–20 mins

Ingredients

115 g/4 oz butter, softened, or soft margarine

115 g/4 oz caster sugar

2 tsp rose water

2 large eggs, lightly beaten

115 g/4 oz self-raising flour

TO DECORATE

115 g/4 oz pink ready-to-roll fondant icing

85 g/3 oz white ready-to-roll fondant icing

85 g/3 oz blue ready-to-roll fondant icing

tube of yellow writing icing

175 g/6 oz unsalted butter, softened

6 tbsp double cream

350 g/12 oz icing sugar, plus extra for dusting

green food colouring

Method

1 Preheat the oven to 180°C/350°F/ Gas Mark 4. Line a 12-hole muffin tin with 8 paper cases.

2 Place the butter, caster sugar and rose water in a large bowl and beat together until light and fluffy. Gradually beat in the eggs. Sift in the flour and, using a metal spoon, fold in gently.

3 Spoon the mixture into the paper cases. Bake in the preheated oven for 15–20 minutes, or until risen, golden and firm to the touch. Transfer to a wire rack and leave to cool.

4 To decorate, roll out the pink fondant icing to a thickness of 5 mm/¼ inch on a surface lightly dusted with icing sugar. Using a small butterfly cutter, stamp out 16 butterflies. Roll out the white and blue fondant icings to the same thickness and, using a small daisy cutter, stamp out about 40 flowers, re-rolling the icing as necessary. Use the yellow writing icing to pipe centres in the flowers.

5 Place the butter, in a bowl and beat with an electric mixer for 2–3 minutes, until pale and creamy. Beat in the cream, then gradually sift in the icing sugar and continue beating for 2–3 minutes, until the buttercream is light and fluffy. Beat in a little green food colouring to give a light green colour.

6 Spoon the buttercream into a large piping bag fitted with a large star nozzle. Pipe swirls of buttercream on top of each cupcake. Decorate with the fondant butterflies and flowers.

Chocolate Mint Cake Pops

🧁 MAKES
28

🥣 PREP TIME
1 hour, plus setting

🧤 COOK TIME
10 mins

Ingredients

300 g/10½ oz plain chocolate,
roughly chopped

25 g/1 oz unsalted butter,
softened

50 g/1¾ oz hard-boiled
mint sweets

450 g/1 lb milk chocolate

50 g/1¾ oz mini marshmallows,
roughly chopped

28 lolly sticks

chocolate sprinkles, to decorate

Method

1 Line a baking tray with baking paper.
Put the plain chocolate in a heatproof
bowl, set the bowl over a saucepan of
gently simmering water and heat until
melted. Stir in the butter. Leave until
the mixture is cool but not beginning
to set.

2 Put the mint sweets in a polythene
bag and tap firmly with a rolling
pin until they are broken into tiny
pieces. Finely chop 150 g/5½ oz of
the milk chocolate, then stir it into
the melted plain chocolate with
the mints and marshmallows until
thoroughly mixed.

3 As soon as the mixture is firm enough
to hold its shape, roll 20 g/¾ oz of it
into a ball. Shape the remaining cake
pops in the same way. Place them
on the baking tray and chill for
30–60 minutes, until firm but not
brittle. Push a lolly stick into each
cake pop, then chill for 10 minutes.

4 Roughly chop the remaining milk
chocolate and melt as above, then
remove from the heat. Dip a cake pop
into the chocolate, turning it until
coated. Lift it from the bowl, letting
the excess drip back into the bowl,
and place it in a cup or tumbler.

Sprinkle with chocolate sprinkles.
Repeat with the remaining cake
pops. Chill or leave in a cool place
until the chocolate has set.

Birthday Party Cupcakes

MAKES 24

PREP TIME 40 mins, plus cooling

COOK TIME 15–20 mins

Ingredients

225 g/8 oz soft margarine

225 g/8 oz caster sugar

4 eggs

225 g/8 oz self-raising flour, sifted

a variety of small sweets and chocolates, sugar-coated chocolates, dried fruit, edible sugar flower shapes, cake decorating sprinkles, sugar strands, and hundreds and thousands

candles and candleholders (optional)

FROSTING

175 g/6 oz butter, softened

350 g/12 oz icing sugar

Method

1 Preheat the oven to 180°C/350°F/ Gas Mark 4. Line two x 12-hole muffin tins with 24 paper cases.

2 Put the margarine, sugar, eggs and flour in a large bowl and, using an electric handheld whisk, beat together until just smooth. Spoon the mixture into the paper cases.

3 Bake the cupcakes in the preheated oven for 15–20 minutes, or until well risen, golden and firm to the touch. Transfer to a wire rack and leave to cool.

4 To make the frosting, put the butter in a bowl and beat until fluffy. Sift in the icing sugar and beat together until smooth and creamy. Spoon the frosting into a piping bag fitted with a large star nozzle. When the cupcakes are cold, pipe circles of frosting on top of each cupcake, then decorate to your choice. If desired, place a candle in the top of each.

Be my Valentine Whoopie Pies

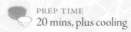

🧁 MAKES
14

🥣 PREP TIME
20 mins, plus cooling

🧤 COOK TIME
35 mins

Ingredients

250 g/9 oz plain flour
1 tsp bicarbonate of soda
large pinch of salt
115 g/4 oz butter, softened
150 g/5½ oz caster sugar
1 large egg, beaten

1 tsp vanilla extract
150 ml/5 fl oz buttermilk
¼ tsp edible red liquid
food colouring
2 tbsp pink heart-shaped
sugar sprinkles

**VANILLA
BUTTERCREAM**

150 g/5½ oz unsalted butter,
softened
1 tsp vanilla extract
4 tbsp double cream
280 g/10 oz icing sugar, sifted

ICING

150 g/5½ oz icing sugar
1–2 tbsp warm water
few drops edible red liquid
food colouring

Method

1 Preheat the oven to 180°C/350°F/
Gas Mark 4. Line two to three large
baking sheets with greaseproof
paper. Sift together the plain flour,
bicarbonate of soda and salt.

2 Place the butter and sugar in a
large bowl and beat with an electric
handheld whisk until pale and
fluffy. Beat in the egg and vanilla
extract followed by half of the flour
mixture then the buttermilk and food
colouring. Stir in the rest of the flour
mixture and mix until thoroughly
incorporated.

3 Pipe or spoon 28 mounds of the
mixture onto the prepared baking
sheets, spaced well apart to allow for
spreading. Bake in the preheated oven,
one sheet at a time, for 9–11 minutes
until risen and just firm to the touch.
Cool for 5 minutes then using a palette
knife transfer to a wire rack and leave
to cool completely.

4 For the vanilla buttercream, place the
butter and vanilla extract in a bowl
and beat with an electric handheld
whisk for 2–3 minutes until pale
and creamy. Beat in the cream then
gradually beat in the icing sugar and
continue beating for 2–3 minutes.

5 For the icing, sift the icing sugar into a
bowl and stir in enough water to make
a smooth icing that is thick enough to
coat the back of a wooden spoon. Beat
in a few drops of food colouring
to colour the icing pale pink.

6 To assemble, spread or pipe the
vanilla buttercream on the flat side
of half of the cakes. Top with the
rest of the cakes. Spoon the icing
over the whoopie pies and decorate
with the heart-shaped sugar
sprinkles. Leave to set.

Traditional Easter Biscuits

MAKES
30

PREP TIME
20 mins, plus cooling

COOK TIME
15 mins

Ingredients

225 g/8 oz butter, softened

140 g/5 oz caster sugar,
plus extra for sprinkling

1 egg yolk, lightly beaten

280 g/10 oz plain flour

1 tsp mixed spice

pinch of salt

1 tbsp mixed peel

55 g/2 oz currants

1 egg white, lightly beaten

Method

1 Place the butter and sugar in a large bowl and beat together until light and fluffy, then beat in the egg yolk. Sift together the flour, mixed spice and salt into the mixture, add the mixed peel and currants and stir until thoroughly combined. Halve the dough, shape into balls, wrap in clingfilm and chill in the refrigerator for 30–60 minutes.

2 Preheat the oven to 190°C/375°F/ Gas Mark 5. Line three large baking sheets with baking paper.

3 Unwrap the dough and roll out between two sheets of baking paper. Cut out biscuits with a 6-cm/2½-inch fluted round cutter and place them on the baking sheets, spaced well

apart. Bake in the preheated oven for 7 minutes, then brush with the egg white and sprinkle with the sugar. Bake for a further 5–8 minutes, or until light golden brown. Leave to cool on the baking sheets for 5–10 minutes, then transfer to wire racks to cool completely.

1

3

3

Anniversary Cupcakes

 MAKES
24

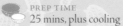 **PREP TIME**
25 mins, plus cooling

 COOK TIME
15–20 mins

Ingredients

225 g/8 oz butter, softened

225 g/8 oz caster sugar

1 tsp vanilla extract

4 large eggs, lightly beaten

225 g/8 oz self-raising flour, sifted

5 tbsp milk

FROSTING

175 g/6 oz unsalted butter

350 g/12 oz icing sugar

25 g/1 oz silver or gold dragées
(cake decoration balls)

Method

1 Preheat the oven to 180°C/350°F/ Gas Mark 4. Line two x 12-hole muffin tins with 24 paper cases.

2 Put the butter, sugar and vanilla extract in a bowl and beat together until light and fluffy. Gradually add the eggs, beating well after each addition. Add the flour and, using a large metal spoon, fold into the mixture with the milk. Spoon the mixture into the paper cases.

3 Bake the cupcakes in the preheated oven for 15–20 minutes, or until well risen and firm to the touch. Transfer to a wire rack and leave to cool.

4 To make the frosting, put the butter in a bowl and beat until fluffy. Sift in the icing sugar and beat together. Put the frosting in a piping bag, fitted with a star-shaped nozzle.

5 When the cupcakes are cold, pipe circles of frosting on top of each cupcake to cover the tops. Sprinkle over the silver or gold dragées before serving.

Wedding Day Fancy Favours

 MAKES
12

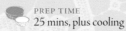 PREP TIME
25 mins, plus cooling

 COOK TIME
15–20 mins

Ingredients

115 g/4 oz butter, softened

100 g/3½ oz caster sugar

2 eggs, lightly beaten

140 g/5 oz self-raising flour, sifted

½ tsp vanilla extract

1–2 tbsp milk

TOPPING

icing sugar, for dusting

225 g/8oz white ready-to-roll fondant icing

3 tbsp runny honey, warmed

2–3 drops pink food colouring

tube of green writing icing

Method

1 Preheat the oven to 200°C/400°F/ Gas Mark 6. Line a 12-hole muffin tin with 12 paper cases. Place the butter and caster sugar into a bowl and beat together until pale and creamy. Gradually add the eggs and continue beating. Fold in the flour using a metal spoon. Stir in the vanilla extract and milk.

2 Spoon the mixture into the paper cases. Bake in the preheated oven for 15–20 minutes, or until well risen and firm to the touch. Transfer to a wire rack and leave to cool.

3 Dust the work surface with icing sugar. Roll out all but one eighth of the fondant icing to 20 x 28 cm/ 8 x 11 inches. Use a biscuit cutter to stamp out 12 rounds. Brush the cake tops with honey and stick on the rounds.

4 For the rosebuds, knead the remaining icing with the food colouring. Roll out 12 strips of icing to 1 x 6 cm/½ x 2½ inches. Roll up and stick on top with honey. Draw on a stalk with the writing icing. Leave to set.

Party Ideas

At a smaller gathering set a place at the table for each person and at a larger party go for a buffet style, arranging a sideboard with party food. Batches of smaller cakes are perfect for larger gatherings, allowing people to eat with their fingers.

Many online websites supply and deliver linen, china and cutlery. Consider charity shops and car boot sales too. Dress the table using flowers suitable to the occasion – dusty pink roses and hydrangeas for afternoon tea or bright delphiniums and snapdragons in different-sized jugs and vases at a summer party.

Tie napkins with ribbon matched to your floral arrangement, add place-names clipped to wine or champagne glasses and set tea-lights in jars. For a grander affair, lay the table with your best linen, set tapering candles into multiple candelabra and look for unique items like old-fashioned comport glasses, which have a wide rim perfect for filling with sweets. Layered glass cake stands lend height and a sense of occasion.

Most importantly, remember to have fun and add the touches that you, personally, love. If you've put a little of yourself into the planning, your guests can't fail to be charmed.

Halloween Mud Pie

SERVES
8

PREP TIME
30 mins, plus cooling

COOK TIME
40 mins

Ingredients

85 g/3 oz plain chocolate

85 g/3 oz unsalted butter

85 g/3 oz light muscovado sugar

2 eggs, beaten

100 ml/3½ fl oz single cream

1 tsp vanilla extract

PASTRY

175 g/6 oz plain flour, plus extra for dusting

25 g/1 oz cocoa powder

40 g/1½ oz light muscovado sugar

85 g/3 oz unsalted butter

2–3 tbsp cold water

TOPPING

250 ml/9 fl oz whipping cream

85 g/3 oz plain chocolate

Method

1 Preheat the oven to 200°C/400°F/ Gas Mark 6. To make the pastry, sift the flour and cocoa powder into a bowl and stir in the sugar. Rub in the butter with your fingertips until the mixture resembles fine breadcrumbs. Add just enough water to bind to a dough.

2 Roll out the dough on a lightly floured work surface to a round large enough to line a 20-cm/8-inch, 3-cm/1¼-inch deep flan tin. Use the pastry to line the tin. Prick the base with a fork, cover with a piece of greaseproof paper and fill with baking beans, then blind-bake the base in the preheated oven for 10 minutes. Remove from the oven and take out the greaseproof paper and beans. Reduce the oven temperature to 180°C/350°F/ Gas Mark 4.

3 Put the chocolate and butter into a saucepan and heat over a low heat, stirring, until melted. Put the sugar and eggs into a bowl and whisk together until smooth, then stir in the chocolate mixture, cream and vanilla extract.

4 Pour the chocolate mixture into the pastry case and bake in the oven for 20–25 minutes, or until just set. Leave to cool.

5 To make the topping, whip the cream until it just holds its shape, then spread over the pie. Melt the chocolate in a bowl set over a saucepan of simmering water, making sure the bowl doesn't come in contact with the water, then spoon into a piping bag and pipe decorations over the cream. Serve cold.

Christmas Macaroons

 MAKES
16

 PREP TIME
30 mins, plus standing

 COOK TIME
10–15 mins

Ingredients

75 g/2¾ oz ground almonds

115 g/4 oz icing sugar

1 tsp ground mixed spice

2 large egg whites

50 g/1¾ oz golden caster sugar

½ tsp freshly grated nutmeg

1 tsp gold dragées

FILLING

55 g/2 oz unsalted butter, softened

juice and finely grated rind of ½ orange

1 tsp ground mixed spice

115 g/4 oz icing sugar, sifted

25 g/1 oz glacé cherries, finely chopped

Method

1 Place the ground almonds, icing sugar and mixed spice in a food processor and process for 15 seconds. Sift the mixture into a bowl. Line two baking sheets with greaseproof paper.

2 Place the egg whites in a large bowl and whisk until they hold soft peaks. Gradually whisk in the caster sugar to make a firm, glossy meringue. Using a spatula, fold the almond mixture into the meringue one third at a time. When all the dry ingredients are thoroughly incorporated, continue to cut and fold the mixture until it forms a shiny batter with a thick, ribbon-like consistency.

3 Pour the mixture into a piping bag fitted with a 1-cm/½-inch plain nozzle. Pipe 32 small rounds onto the prepared baking sheets. Tap the baking sheets firmly onto a work surface to remove air bubbles. Sprinkle half the macaroons with the grated nutmeg and gold dragées. Leave at room temperature for 30 minutes. Meanwhile, preheat the oven to 160°C/325°F/Gas Mark 3.

4 Bake in the preheated oven for 10–15 minutes. Cool for 10 minutes, then carefully peel the macaroons off the greaseproof paper. Leave to cool completely.

5 To make the filling, beat the butter and orange juice and rind in a bowl until fluffy. Gradually beat in the mixed spice and icing sugar until smooth and creamy. Fold in the glacé cherries. Use to sandwich pairs of macaroons together.